C000071815

GETTING OVER AN AFFAIR

5 Big Secrets Experts Want You To Know On How To Deal With Your Partner's Infidelity

JULIE ROSE

Copyright © 2017

All rights reserved.

ISBN: 9781520357577

TEXT COPYRIGHT © [JULIE ROSE]

all rights reserved. No part of this guide may be reproduced in any form without permission in writing from the publisher except in the case of brief quotations embodied in critical articles or reviews.

Legal & disclaimer

The information contained in this book and its contents is not designed to replace or take the place of any form of medical or professional advice; and is not meant to replace the need for independent medical, financial, legal or other professional advice or services, as may be required. The content and information in this book have been provided for educational and entertainment purposes only.

The content and information contained in this book have been compiled from sources deemed reliable, and it is accurate to the best of the author's knowledge, information, and belief. However, the author cannot guarantee its accuracy and validity and cannot be held liable for any errors and/or omissions. Further, changes are periodically made to this book as and when needed. Where appropriate and/or necessary, you must consult a professional (including but not limited to your doctor, attorney, financial advisor or such other professional advisor) before using any of the suggested remedies, techniques, or information in this book.

Upon using the contents and information contained in this book, you agree to hold harmless the author from and against any damages, costs, and expenses, including any legal fees potentially resulting from the application of any of the information provided by this book. This disclaimer applies to any loss, damages or injury caused by the use and application, whether directly or indirectly, of any advice or information presented, whether for breach of contract, tort, negligence, personal injury, criminal intent, or under any other cause of action.

You agree to accept all risks of using the information presented inside this book.

You agree that by continuing to read this book, where appropriate and/or necessary, you shall consult a professional (including but not limited to your doctor, attorney, or financial advisor or such other advisor as needed) before using any of the suggested remedies, techniques, or information in this book.

TABLE OF CONTENT

INTRODUCTION

I want to thank you and congratulate you for downloading the book *"Getting Over An Affair: 5 Big Secrets Experts Want You To Know On How To Deal With Your Partner's Infidelity"*

Everyone knows that marriage is sacred; it binds two people to each other. Each person begins with high hopes and vows an everlasting love to the other person. They wish to live together until death comes for them. They involve in a lot of promises and even more compromises. They share the same love that is so strong they have decided to bind it and make a union.

However, in the society nowadays, finding a true love seems very impossible. Relationships aren't always certain and everlasting as they seem to be. No one is perfect and none of them seems to believe in living happily ever after anymore. People are more willing to believe in break-ups, misfortunes, and sad love stories than a love that withstands all the obstacles and stay the same. This affects the concept of marriage greatly. A lot of married couples decide to annul, divorce or be separated from each other. They cannot seem to keep the love and end up leaving the person they had once promised forever to.

As sad as this is, what is even worse is that some people decides to cheat on the very person they promised to spend the rest of their life with and hurt them. Separating due to indifference or not having time enough with each other seems reasonable but to separate because of a third party seems irresponsible. How would you know if your partner is cheating on you and what are you going to do if you have found out about the cheating? How are you going to be able to deal with it? This book will help you to get through it if it ever comes that time comes.

Thank you again for purchasing this book, and I hope you enjoy it!

SECRET 1 – CATCHING THE CHEATING SPOUSE

Marriage is a hard thing to keep especially with the temptations outside of it. Most of the times, one of the couple ends up getting hurt and there are a lot of reasons to why this is happening. Affairs are the most common reasons why marriages end and why it is very hard to keep your spouse. What are you going to do when you caught your spouse cheating on you? How to handle it and how to find out? Here are some tips on this matter.

How To How To Find Out Your Spouse's Affair

As a woman, you are bound to have this intuition on whether your husband is cheating on you or not. This goes vice versa but the point is when you have a gut feeling that your spouse is lying to you on purpose, find out if the feeling is true. Do not just let it go? After all, you have got nothing to lose on finding it out. No matter how much you trust your partner, there will be times when you will have doubts and the only way to resolve it is by finding out the truth. If you think there is a possibility of your partner cheating on you, then it's time for you to start finding out the signs of that he is being unfaithful. Take action immediately. The longer you procrastinate coping with this situation, the worse you will feel if you find out he is a cheating spouse. If you want to know whether or not your partner is cheating on you, then you should look at what he acts around you, pay more attention to what he has changed suddenly. Here is a list of signs revealing that your spouse has not been honest with you and having an affair with someone else.

The Top 14 Signs Reveal that Your Spouse is Cheating

1. Always dressing up or caring physical appearance

Have you noticed a sudden change in your beloved's attire? Is your spouse looking a little better or with a little more fashion sense? Try to see if your partner is looking a whole lot sophisticated than usual. If it seems that the love of your life is paying more attention to appearances, he begins to use nice perfume, buy new clothes but never wear them before you. The spouse begins to work out more often, spend more time caring his physical appearance. This should send you an alarm signal, especially if your partner is not the type to suddenly do so. He may be trying to look good to someone else.

2. Spend less time with you

Your partner usually comes home late after work or keeps working longer hours. When you try to contact and ask why they will be home late, they tend to give you vague answers or pretend that *"they couldn't hear the phone since they are in the meeting or they are meeting a business partner"* blah blah …

3. Become more distant or distracted

If he is usually caring, supportive, attentive to you, always beside you, asks you how your day is, loves to hang out with you, become interested in having conversations with you about jobs, life, children, and then they suddenly seem more distant or distracted from you. They may lose interest in family activities, instead, they prefer to spend more time on their phone or computer. This may be a sign revealing that they are cheating on you.

4. Guards the phone, computer all the time

When the one you promised to spend the rest of your life seems to keep on checking the phone or computer, making sure it is out of your reach. For example: when you walk by or enter his room, he tends to turn off the phone or computer immediately. This is a sign helps you can suspect that he becomes secretive. Your partner might just be hiding something from you. Of course, you cannot be sure that it is another person it can be just a big surprise or something but it is most definitely suspicious. Even if you cannot look into the phone or computer, this simple sign is something to take note of.

Remember, you have promised each other that you will share everything, so you might want to think about the reason that the phone is heavily guarded. When your betrothed is hiding something from you, it is usually a bad sign.

5. Keeps everything with a password

Besides the phone, is there anything else that your spouse seems to protect dearly? You will find it out by borrowing that object. For example, try borrowing that person's laptop and just say that you are going to check your email or some believable excuse. Check if things are password protected.

What does it mean if all the gadgets at your house that belong to the one you are involved with have a password? For all you know, what is in there could be something that will potentially ruin your marriage.

6. Become defensive

Your partner becomes a bit confused, hesitant or gets defensive when you ask about his day or night out with the men or ladies. This may be a sign of cheating.

7. Having arguments with you

A cheating spouse may try to make you feel down, feel guilty as if you have done something wrong to him. They usually become angry with you easily, start fights, arguments or even accuse you of cheating on them.

8. Gets new credit cards

Another sign an affair is in action is when a new credit card is taken on by your partner. Think about it, what could possibly be the reason why there is a need for a new credit card that you cannot monitor unless it is for letting someone else use it without letting you know.

This is one of the surest signs that your spouse is having an affair: When money is spent for someone you do not know. The more secretive your partner is, the more suspicious you should become.

9. Begins making hurtful remarks

When the love of your life begins on making hurtful comments about you or trying to pass it off as a joke, this can be interpreted as a lack of interest in you. Worse is that they might be done on purpose for the sake of getting you mad. The worst thing is that the snide remarks and hurtful comment might just be the true feelings of your partner.

10. Always talk about a certain someone

If your other half tends to drop a name into a conversation, always, without doing it on purpose and even when you keep on noticing it, something is terribly wrong. This can somehow mean that these certain someone is always on your spouse's mind. A slip of the tongue is usually how criminals get caught. So if your special person is always saying a certain someone's name or telling you stories about that someone, beware because this might be the person you should be careful about.

11. Talks bad about a certain person

If by chance, your beloved talks bad about a certain person and it seem to you that it is done on purpose, think again. Talking bad about a specific person can be a sign of covering up any traces of affection. Do not let this fool you, be wary of your spouse and make sure that this person and your spouse are totally not connected in any romantic way. Try your best to ask around or investigate on this to confirm your suspicions.

12. Suggests separate holidays

Couples usually spend holidays together since they consider this as a bonding time, somewhat. So if for instance, your spouse suddenly suggests that you should have separate holidays, this can also translate to him spending the holidays with someone else. It might be good not to let your spouse do this and see how he would react to that. If he gets annoyed and acts mad during the holidays, then you have proven to yourself that your spouse is really having an affair with someone else.

13. Doesn't want physical intimacy

Sex is pretty much a vital part in a marriage and sometimes it is one of the things that hold a relationship together. When your partner always come up with an excuse not to have sex with you, this should be alarming. After all, making love with your partner means that there is a love shared between the two of you. What are the reasons your spouse does not want to make love to you anymore? One of them could be that he is having an affair and is getting the sex he wants with someone else and does not feel the need to do it with you any longer. They may become less intimate or affectionate, or they may not feel distant even when you do have sex. Your spouse might no longer give you a hug or a sweet kiss or even he doesn't want to hold your hands like he used to

14. Flirt on social media

Social media is totally one of the best ways to check if your spouse is having an affair. Most of the time, people do not bother with separating their personal lives with their social media account so traces of an affair may be pretty obvious if you try checking it out. Look for someone that is always liking your spouse's photos or commenting on it or maybe posting on his or her wall. This can be a sign that he is having an affair with this person or that they are totally close.

Of course, these are just signs to help you know if your spouse is having an affair or not. It can still be wrong but if you got all the signs, you might want to look farther into it.

Staying Calm And Collect The Evidence While Confronting A Cheater

Once you have a suspicion that your spouse is a cheater and you have gotten something you can use to prove it. You need to stay calm and collect evidence. Following is a list of ways help you to find out if your partner is a cheater:

1. Wait until your spouse is sleeping or being in the bathroom. Quietly check his phone and computer. Be careful or you will get caught. Have a look at his call history and messages. Pay attention to names or numbers that seems strange. You can also check his Facebook, Zalo, Viber, Skype or Twitter. Find out if any conversations he has contacted new people. Likewise, you can check his web browsing history if you can access to his computer.

2. You can hire a private investigator who is licensed to do a task of catching your cheating spouse if your financial status is good enough. This, of course, is a great way, even the best way to find out if your partner is cheating you or not.

3. You can quietly download a cell phone spying software on your spouse's phone. Your partner absolutely will not see this app once it is downloaded and set up. This app will allow you detect all your spouse's messages, emails, phone contacts, web browsing history, and so on.

4. You can track your partner by installing a GPS device in his vehicle, clothing or bag. It will let you know where he driving to, how far it is from your place to his place.

5. You can secretly follow your spouse if you suspect that he is going to meet up with his lover. Make sure that you keep a safe distance from your spouse when you are driving or walking. Bring binoculars along with you so you can see your partner from far away. You may hire someone else to drive you if possible so you can pay full attention to him easily.

6. You can plan a surprise visit to his office unnoticed. As if you pretend to show your care to him like you bring him a lunch box. This way may also help you catch your cheating spouse.

7. You can provide him an excuse that you are going to the hair salon or meeting up with a friend, and then you track him from your spying devices to see if your partner uses your absence as a great chance to meet up with someone else.

Confronting your partner

It isn't pleasant at all when you find out that your spouse has been cheating on you. Stay calm! you have the upper hand, no need for you to get aggravated. Relax and start the confrontation with a poker face, present to him your concrete proof. It would be hard and awkward if you approach your cheating spouse without any concrete evidence. The evidence you collected may include text messages, voice messages, emails, photos, videos. Once you bring these all evidence to your partner, make sure they must be logical and force him to have to accept the truth, don't let him refuse your things or convince that you misunderstood him, made mistakes or even tell that you are crazy. Never allow your cheating spouse explain their unfaithful behaviors. Remember that you should not reveal the cheater about your source of evidence. This way will avoid the situation that he will become more careful in using his phone and computer. He may change the passwords, delete cookies and caches in web history, delete text messages, photos, videos or even he may change his routines suddenly so that you would not find out his affair easily.

Listen To The Counsels

Now you know that your spouse has cheated on you, an annoying feeling will wash over you. You may suffer from negative emotions or traumatic experiences like you eat too much, you can't sleep, you cannot concentrate on your work, lose your trust to your partner and even feel hopeless about your marriage. Your spouse has made a choice and you are left to cope with it. What are you going to do to be able to cope with the fact that your spouse cheated on you? Well, you can try to get some counseling from a psychologist or a counselor to explain what you are going through and what action you can take or you can talk to a friend so you can lighten the burden you carry in your heart. All in all, you need to find an ear that will listen to you. This will keep you stay calm and become stronger.

Now, it's time for you to decide if you are going to remain with your spouse or leave him. The next Secret will help you with that.

SECRET 2 – TO SACRIFICE OR TO LET THE CHEATER GO

Your spouse is cheating on you and you are unsure of what you are going to do. Should you stay or should you go? Truly, that is the biggest question that would be bothering you as of the moment. Do not worry because no matter how hard it is to decide on that, this Secret will help you to figure out what your heart has to say regarding this matter.

What Is Really Happening In Your Relationship?

Cheating is an offense that is unforgivable especially when it is not the first time someone is caught doing it. Is this your partner's first time to cheat on you? How does cheating affect the relationship you have with the love of your life? Well, when a person cheats on another, the trust that is shared between the two of you becomes damaged.

It is very hard to gain a person's trust and almost impossible to regain it once it is lost. What happens in a relationship when the other one cheats are that it deteriorates until nothing is left of the marriage. Cheating is going to ruin all the years that the married couple has gone through together and leave each individual with nothing to return to. Each person suffers but the one who is left trying to fix the relationship suffers the most because it is like trying to fix a broken vase and he might just get his finger cut in the process.

The Spouse's Affair Is Not Your Fault – 7 Shocking Reasons

Do you think that it is your fault? Well, think again. Here are 5 shocking reasons why you are not the one to blame for your betrothed's affair.

1. Sometimes, it's the marriage

As the marriage progresses, the bond shared between the two persons can weaken or strengthen. Due to the limitless temptations out there, most of the marriages tend to weaken. Problems with the kids, the house, the in-laws, the money, the job, the car and much more tend to come up until there is no more room for mistakes. Both parties feel as if they are under pressure and when they give up and stop supporting each other on fighting back to these problems, that moment is when their marriage fails. If your marriage fails, you really cannot blame yourself if he cheats on you.

2. High expectations

Another reason that your other half feels the need to cheat on you might be that he has set the bar high. Expectations that are not fulfilled by you can be why he tries to find it in someone else. Most of the times, you do not know what these expectations are so you do not know how to meet them. If this is the case, then it is most definitely not your fault that your spouse is cheating because he is the one who expected too much without saying anything at all.

3. Mostly, it's just mid-life crisis

Most adults tend to have this so called mid-life crisis where they try to relive their younger days, most especially their glory days. They want to go back to their past life and so they want a younger partner or someone young to be with them. If this is the cause of his cheating, then it is most definitely not your fault. Not all people are strong enough to get through this crisis and end up spending most of his or her life at this stage. Be happy that it is not you going through it.

4. Maybe it's lack of maturity

Love and marriage must come hand in hand and that is why it is very difficult to keep a marriage. Sometimes, there will be problems that both parties must understand to be able to keep the relationship. The problem is most of the time, the other person is not mature enough to deal with the obstacles of a relationship. Because of this, arguments and fights arise until both individuals are just too tired to talk to each other and just wants to be left alone. In their alone state, one of them will try to find comfort in someone else's arms and cheating then happens.

5. Family history of divorce or infidelity

Find out if your spouse has parents, ancestors or any other close relatives who had affairs. If your partner used to witness infidelity among those members since they were at a young age, they are much more likely to be influenced and become a cheater to their partner when they grow up.

6. Friends

Find out if most of your spouse's friends are married already or still single. Studies show that people tend to involve in infidelity if they spend much time with their social circles, those who are mostly single and have affairs with someone else. Sooner or later he will be welcomed into that circle and become a cheating spouse.

7. Social media

With the ease of the internet and smart phones, your spouse will have more chance to communicate with anyone he/she considers to be potential partners. They prefer to have new feelings, new friends or even new lover to share everything with. Therefore, participating in social media will also increase the possibility of affairs happening between your spouse and someone else.

Confronting Your Fears And Doubts

If you are having doubts that he might be cheating on you, do not fear. The best thing to do is to confront these doubts. Trail his car to the workplace or to the place you suspect that they might be meeting or have someone else do it for you. You can also just ask him although he is most likely to deny it.

The best way is to catch him off the guard so that he would be unprepared and unable to cover up the traces of his or her affair. If you can catch him with the person he is having an affair with, then that is even better. Do not be afraid to confirm whether your doubts are true and do not let the fear of knowing control you. Remember that there is power in knowledge and the only way to get the upper hand is to know exactly what is going on.

Stepping Up: Should You Still Stay?

Once your fears and doubts are confirmed and you have found out that the person you have trusted the most is cheating on you, what are you going to do? Are you going to leave or are you going to stay? You need to think about it thoroughly. Is there a reason why you must stay and forgive him for doing this to you? Do you still want to try to make your marriage work? Is he willing to promise never to do it again and remain loyal to you from that day onwards? Are you willing to believe his or her promise? Do you think that you might be able to give your trust again?

By answering these questions, you are bound to have decided whether or not you are going to stay. Just keep in mind that whatever your decision may be, it should be the one that your heart and mind agrees on. The next Secret will tell you if a cheater will always be a cheater and enlighten you on the word: trust. So go to the next Secret and find out more about this.

SECRET 3 – THE REAL PROBLEMS OF THE AFFAIR

Once you have quite an idea on whether you should stay or go, the next thing to ask yourself is if a cheater will always be a cheater. Will your spouse still commit the same mistake even after he has promised you that the first time he cheated would be the last one as well? Is the temptation too much that he has succumbed to it?

Why Is Your Spouse Cheating On You?

There are tons of reasons why your other half can be lying to you. It could be that he is just tired of living with someone else and want to be left out on his or her own. Maybe he fell out of love with you; it could be as simple as that or as complicated as him having a problem with you that you do not know about. What should you be able to do? It is going to be so hard during the first time but you are going to get through this. What are the common reasons why he is cheating on you? The next part will discuss some of them.

The Top 10 Reasons Why Your Partner Becomes A Cheater

Cheating has been going on for a very long time in the society. It is something that is very hard to stop as trust is lost during the process. What do you do to prevent the one you have made your vows with from deceiving you and finding someone else to love? The answer is simple: you need to consider the reasons why people are deceiving their partners and try to fulfill them.

1. Not satisfied with partner in a sexual manner

Men love to experiment especially with sexuality. They want to explore and look for their limits. Women, on the other hand, tend to be more laid back on that topic. People have a different hunger for sexual desires and if you do not want your partner to cheat on you, what you need to do is figure out if they are sexually satisfied with your relationship. If you can fulfill that, you might be able to prevent him from lying to you. Sex is a very vital part in most relationships so you need to keep this in consideration.

2. Wishes to engage with others sexually

Sometimes, one partner is not enough for a person and after years of settling down, suddenly the person gets an urge to engage sexually with another person. The person wants to get another feeling or is searching for something different than his wife. This sort of reason as to why he is having an affair with someone else cannot be easily resolved. Can you willingly let your husband have sex with someone else as long as he is not romantically involved with that person? If you are then, this should be easily resolved; the problem arises if you are not willing to go through that.

3.   Not satisfied with emotional support from partner

Your husband/wife is your main source of emotional support, he is the one who you expect to give you advice, comfort you whenever you feel sad, be there for you when it seems that the whole world is against you and love you unconditionally. Sadly, there are times that your partner seems to lack the emotional support you are searching for and you feel that you need to seek it from someone else. He might feel the same way and try to look for that support from another person. If you want to stop him from going in another direction, then be more supportive and understanding of him and let him know that you are enough.

4.   Wants to be appreciated with another person

Sometimes, your other half feels that your appreciation of the thing he does is not enough. As if you do not express it enough or he does not feel it at all. You need to be more expressive, you need to show your spouse that every simple thing he does, you appreciate more than ever. If you do appreciate it and it seems that he seems to be looking for more, then it is not a problem with you anymore, just that he thinks that your appreciation for the things he has done is not enough and he wants more.

5.   Fell out of love

As the marriage progress, people tend to lose the interest they once had in their partner. Love is such a big word and you have both promised to love each other for the rest of your lives but a person is always capable of loving another person. At some point, maybe the lowest point of your marriage, your husband might find another person to love and in the process fall out of love with you. Of course, the love he has for you will always be there but it can certainly be overshadowed by another. When he falls out of love with you, the only way to solve it is to make him fall in love with you all over again.

6. Wants to get revenge on partner

If you have ever cheated on your partner before and he knows about it, there is a high chance that he is doing the same to you only because he wants to seek revenge on you. Your husband wants you to know how he felt when you were the one doing it and wants to make you suffer for it. After all, the best way to get revenge on someone is to ask for an eye for an eye that was lost. Since trust is gone between the two of you, he finds it easier to cheat on you.

7. Wants to have new experiences

There are also times when your partner is simply tired of how the two of you are living, he may be bored and want to have new experiences with another person. Because marriage becomes stagnant after so many years, it is certainly possible that your want for adventure might decrease while your partner is still searching for a thrill, danger and something like that. When this happens, he might want to seek it from someone else if it seems that you cannot give it.

8. Lack of intimacy and attention

Do you not have the same way of showing your affection as you did before? Has time changed the way you intimately talk with each other or touch each other? Do you not have the time to spare for your husband anymore and you do not even give him enough attention? If so, then you really cannot blame him if he cheats on you. After all, intimacy and attention are some of a human's basic needs and he seeks that from you, the wife. If the relationship lacks these two, then you must really expect it not to work out.

9. Lack of self-esteem

If your partner is not confident, you will want to find someone who is more confident about himself or herself, someone who is able to stand up for the things that he wants. If you lack self-esteem, keeping your husband might be hard because you will always think that you are not good enough for him and eventually he will get tired of proving to you that you are worth it because he loves you. If you want to keep him and you have a lack of self-esteem, make the love he has for you into something that will help you have more confidence in yourself.

10. Financial problems

Money is one of the worst problems out there and it has ruined a lot of marriages in the past. When the husband or the wife cannot provide enough money for the family and the couple has kids, then things are set out for the worst. You cannot live without enough money to feed your family and it certainly is very hard to keep on loving each other when you are trying to find how you are going to feed yourselves or pay for the bill or prevent your family from getting kicked out of the apartment you are renting in.

Are You Good Enough?

When someone cheats, the person left asks herself over and over again if she is not good enough. Are you thinking that you are not enough for your spouse that your spouse is still looking for someone other than you? Well, the answer is simple: it is not that you are not good enough but he thinks that the new person is way better than you. It is you're his way of thinking and other people are sure to have another point of view on this. Do not let all that is happening to get into your head. It is not that you are not good enough; it could be that your husband is just searching for something else.

At the end of the day, unless a divorce is filed, you are still married to each other and you can still work this out. Will a cheater always be a cheater? Well, the first time could be a mistake but if a second time happens, then that should give you your answer. The next Secret will help you in recovering from the affair so turn to the next page and find out more.

SECRET 4 –RECOVERING, BEING A BETTER OF YOU

After learning from the previous Secret about the most common reasons why your partner might cheat on you, this one will help you to get through this problem. You are the legal wife; you need to remain strong for your family especially if you have kids. Do not let the affair ruin the bond you have with your children. Here are some of the steps you need to take in order to keep your life going.

8 Easy Ways You Can Learn To Recover From the Affair

Once you have figured out about the affair and have confronted your husband, you need to decide on what to do next. If he has told you that he would not do it again, then here are some of the things you can do in order to recover from the affair you have discovered.

1. Talk to your friends

The first thing you can do to at least get all the anger, sadness, fear and your mixed emotions on control is to let them out. Talk it out with your friends so that these heightened emotions might subside. The best thing to do to recover is said your real feelings and let your friends advise you on what you should do or at least let them sympathize with you so you will have the strength to go through another day because having discovered about the affair will surely devastate you.

2. Ask all the questions you want

During another confrontation with your husband, ask him all the things you want to know about the affair he had. Answering all the curious questions inside your head will help you to get over what happened and make you surer of yourself. When nothing else is bothering you, settling down and becoming more calm and strong will be an easier process. It takes courage to discover the truth so show him that you are brave enough to do so. Do not be intimidated that the girl he replaced you with might be prettier and be more confident with yourself.

3. Remain calm all the way

After the affair is done and your husband is on his knees begging for forgiveness, calm down. Do not show any emotions, not fear, not sadness and not even anger or satisfaction. Let him feel the weight of all that he has done to you. Then, remain calm all the way even as you say that you will give him another chance to prove himself and fix the problem that he has made.

4. Set a period to talk about the affair

In order to recover from the affair, you need to accept that it has happened. You need to know how long it has been going on and more details about it. You've asked all the questions you wanted to know about but setting a certain time period so you can talk about your affair would be better. Set some time aside, around 15-20 minutes a day to talk about the affair and nothing else.

5. Expect the release of emotions

You really cannot expect your partner to be as calm as you are. So expect that he might lash out emotions on you that he might suddenly break down in the middle of your confrontations. You need to accept that he is human too and in defending himself, there might be some emotional outbursts that you need to watch out for. Just make sure that he does not overdo himself and does not hurt you in the process.

6. Let him know how it affected you

You are not going to do this to take revenge on him but to be fair and just. You need to tell him how you felt during the times that he was cheating on you, especially the moment that you caught him in the act of doing it. Tell your side of the story and be as honest as possible. Do not exaggerate just to make your husband suffer more. Be truthful and explain to him in the best way possible that the affair he was in has affected you in a lot of ways and has changed the way you look at him, the way you see him and the effects it has inflicted on your family.

7. Do not easily forgive your partner

Just because he begged for your forgiveness while he was down on his knees make it right for you to forgive your husband. He still cheated on you and that is real. Let him know that you are mad at him for the wrongs he has done and he needs to make it up to you. Do not easily be swayed even if he promises you things that you want to hear. Keep in mind that these words are just empty promises until they are proven true. Tell him that and let your husband reflect on what he has done wrong.

8. Spend time with him without talking about the affair

You can only recover from an affair if it is not on your mind 24/7. Do not always talk about the affair whenever you are with your husband. Spend some time together just like before, go out for dinner, watch some movies, go to parties and such. You need to let him know that although you have not forgiven him just yet, there is a chance that you will and that is all he needs to hold on to save your relationship from dying.

5 Lessons You Will Learn From the Affair

After going through all that hardships, surely, there must be a lot of things that you have learned from it. Knowing that your partner is cheating on you is a very hard thing to take but it comes with a lot of lessons. Here are some things that you can eventually derive from it.

Lesson 1: Infidelity is definitely not your fault

It is definitely not your fault that your husband decided to find someone else to spend his time with and whisper sweet nothings. But if your marriage is failing, you could have made some mistakes as well. So as much as you want to blame your husband for it all, you totally cannot, you have some part of it. Still, though, cheating was his choice and it was one he made all by himself and that is certainly the truth.

Lesson 2: Knowing about an affair changes you

Knowing that your husband cheated takes a piece of your heart and it is forever lost. It will change you, make you feel like you are not enough and that you will never be enough for anyone else. He chose another person over you although he promised to always choose you and that will leave a scar in you that no one would be able to erase. Worry not, because you are a strong woman and surviving this is something that you will do.

Lesson 3: You need to let go if he wants to be set free

Once you have caught him in the act, the first thing he is most likely to do will be to beg for forgiveness especially if you have never been anything but a good wife to him. Sadly, there are also times that a husband asks to be set free. Do not blame yourself for this but know that you need to decide whether you are going to let him go or not. The best thing would be to set him free and let him know that even after all that he has done, you still respect the fact that he is your husband and the love you have for him will be enough to let him go.

Lesson 4: Forgiveness will come eventually

Another thing that you will learn from the affair is that eventually, the wounds will heal and you are going to be able to forgive your husband for the things that he did to you. It takes time, a very long time, but forgiveness will come. It will not sweep you off your feet but it is like small waves that come rushing to your heart and if you still truly love him, you would still want him to be by your side when that moment of forgiveness surges your heart.

Lesson 5: It can be better to be left alone than remain being cheated on

Even though forgiveness will come, the trust you have will still be broken and it is very difficult to keep a relationship without trust. So keep in mind that if you think he is still going to ever cheat on you again, then truly let him go, because it is better to be alone than let him keep on cheating on you over and over again until you truly do not know why you keep on letting him come back to you.

3 Fastest Ways To Restore Your Trust

If you have decided that you will truly let him back to your side, then restore your trust in him is definitely a must. What are the steps you need to take in order to fix that? Below are some of the actions you can try.

1. Forgive him

Now that you have decided to let him in your heart again, then even though it is hard, you need to forgive him for what he has done to you and the things he has put you through. Let go of all the grudges you have and hold on to the fact that he chose to stay with you and has not asked you to set him free. That fact should be enough to make you forgive him.

2. Do not expect anything

If you are expecting that your husband will be extra sweeter to you once you have decided to restore your trust in him, then you are up for a disappointment. Do not expect anything from him and let him do what he wants. You need to keep in mind that sometimes when you least expect anything to happen is the time when he will surprise you with roses, a dinner date and maybe say those three words to you again and again until you believe that he has repented for all that he has done.

3. Put out a little hope

Lastly, as much as you think that he will ever cheat on you again, you need to put out some hope that he is now a changed person. Convince yourself, even a little bit that he would not dare to do it again. Give him the benefit of the doubt and tell yourself that he deserves it at the very least. Maybe things are going to get better, maybe he will decide that you are definitely worth this and repent of all the things he has done.

2 Perfect Ways To Broadcast The Issue

Lastly, in order to assure your spot as the legal wife, you need other people to know about the things that have been going on. These are some of the ways you can retell the story of the affair.

1. Let your parents know

Tell your parents what has happened in a calm and collected manner. Let them know that he had an affair and that he is sorry and wants to find a way to make it up to you. You need a witness that he is changing his ways and this will also help in keeping extra eyes on him whenever you are away on a business trip or something similar to that.

2. Write a blog

Blogs are fantastic. You can choose to let everyone know who you are or make your identity hidden and still be able to tell your story. So if you really want to broadcast the issue, then this would be one of the best media for you. Let your voice be heard and let your emotions pour out. Write an amazing entry or a series of entries worth recollecting for.

Once that you have figured out what you are going to do to remain strong and be the best wife you can be, then the next thing to know would be how you are going to give him a second chance. The next Secret would be able to help you with that so turn to the next page and read on.

SECRET 5 – FORGIVING

Your husband has told you that he is going to do all that he can to prove to you that he has changed and that he is going to be the faithful partner he once was. Are you willing to take the risk and give him another chance? After all, is love not sweeter the second time around? Everyone deserves to have another shot at proving themselves worthy so you should definitely let him have another take on your marriage. Here are some of the things to do when giving your cheating partner another chance.

5 Useful Ways You Should Apply When Giving Your Cheating Spouse A Second Chance

Your spouse has been telling you promises of forever again and you are hooked up with it yet you still carry with you a lot of doubts so this second chance would be like a trial to another forever with him. Here are some of the things you might want to try out in giving him another shot at it.

1. **Go somewhere nice for a vacation**

Get away from the mistress, the place where the cheating has happened and everything that reminds you and him of the affair. Go somewhere far away or someplace with a nice view for an out of season vacation. Maybe you can go out to the beach, out of the country, go travel the world with him and rekindle the love you once had. Maybe during the vacation, you will both realize that you truly love each other and forget all about the affair that has happened.

2. **Let him pamper you**

If he wants to serve you like a queen, cook for you, kiss you every morning when he wakes up, bring you breakfast in bed, chose your clothes for you, hug you every moment he can, get your coat for you, help you settle in your chair, help you carry your luggage, let him. Let him treat you like a queen because you are one and you deserve it. This might be his way of saying that he is sorry and that he is repenting. Or it could just be his way of telling you that he still loves you after all. Let him prove to you that he has changed and that having another affair is something that is most unlikely to happen again.

3. Do not judge him

If he does something that seems wrong to you, do not judge him. Let him still have the freedom to do the things that he wants to do and show him that you love him and that you appreciate the things he has done for you. You cannot keep on judging him for the rest of your relationship because of one mistake that he made and just forget about all the right things he has done.

4. Learn to stop suspecting him

Nothing good ever comes out of suspicions. If you are really going to give him a second chance then you need to forget that the affair ever happened. He can do all the things that he thinks would be good for him, do not keep on watching every move. Do not keep on monitoring all his messages and email. Give him the benefit of the doubt every single time that you think he might be cheating on you again. You are doing this to save your relationship and because you think that he has the capability to change his ways so let him do his part and you do yours.

5. Fall in love all over again

It is not like your love is lost just because he has cheated on you, your love is still there, your trust is just a little bit broken. So think about it, what is the best way you can do to give him a second chance without holding anything back? Simple enough, what you need to do is just fall in love with him again. Fall in love with the way he tries to make it up to you, in the way that he tries his best to prove to you that he still deserves you and the way that he chose to remain on your side.

3 Red Hot Keys To Patch Up Things

Now that you have decided that he is worth another chance, what is left is to patch things up and go back to the love you once shared. Here are some of the tips to ease up and have a smooth sailing to that relationship.

1. Have a talk

Talk about the things that you have been through. Tell him how you saw that he has changed his ways and that you are happy that he is keeping his promise now. Let him know how much you appreciate the fact that he chose to stay with you and save your marriage. It is not easy and he chose to live with that instead of taking the easy way out.

2. Decide on how to make your relationship work

Now that you had the talk, you might as well decide how you are still going to make your relationship work. Are you just going back to the way you were before or create a fresh start? Hear his side as well; do not just keep on babbling the things you want to happen. Be a team in making this decision because you are still a married couple after all.

3. Forget about it

Tell him that the affair does not matter to you anymore right now, as long as he is going to keep the promise of never doing it again. Then, totally forget it, erase the affair from your mind and continue on being with him as if nothing has ever happened and just continue being happy together.

To sum it all up, everyone deserves a second chance and it is never too late to give it to him. If he decided to choose you, then he must be dedicated to keeping his promises and making sure that you are happy. He is entitled to proving himself to you at the very least, so let him.

CONCLUSION

Congratulations on reaching the end of the book!

Truly, knowing that the person you have trusted the most in this world, the love of your life, the person you consider to be your other half has cheated on you will hurt you so bad, crush your soul and make you feel as if the whole world has turned its back on you. You are unsure of what you should do next and you are very devastated. You do not even know if you should give your partner a second chance at proving to you that he is regretful of what he has done.

Nonetheless, you need to be strong, brave and forgiving. If he decides that he wants to stay with you and show you that he is worth it, then for all that matters, give him a second chance at it because everyone deserves a second chance. If after that chance, he engages in an affair once more, then stops. Tell him that he is not worth your time and tell you that you are better off without him.

Do not let this affair affect what you think of yourself because you are beautiful, amazing, and awesome and you are going to survive this. Whatever you decide is the right thing to do, stand by it, fight for it and you will know that marriages are not perfect but if two people are willing to make it work, then by all means, it is definitely worth all the hardships.

Thank you again for downloading this book on *"Getting Over An Affair: 5 Big Secrets Experts Want You To Know On How To Deal With Your Partner's Infidelity"* and reading all the way to the end. I'm extremely grateful.

If you know of anyone else who may benefit from the informative tips presented in this book, please help me inform them of this book. I would greatly appreciate it.

Finally, if you enjoyed this book and feel that it has added value to your life in any way, please take a couple of minutes to share your thoughts and post a REVIEW on Amazon. Your feedback will help me to continue to write the kind of Kindle books that helps you get results. Furthermore, if you write a simple REVIEW with positive words for this book on Amazon, you can help hundreds or perhaps thousands of other readers who may want to enhance their life have a chance getting what they need. Like you, they worked hard for every penny they spend on books. With the information and recommendation you provide, they would be more likely to take action right away. We really look forward to reading your review.

Thanks again for your support and good luck!

If you enjoy my book, please write a POSITIVE REVIEW on amazon.

-- JULIE ROSE--

CHECK OUT OTHER BOOKS

Go here to check out other related books that might interest you:

Daughter of Strife: 7 Techniques On How To Win Back Your Stubborn Teenage Daughter

http://www.amazon.com/dp/B01HS5E3V6

Parenting Teens With Love And Logic: A Survival Guide To Overcoming The Barriers Of Adolescence About Dating, Sex And Substance Abuse

http://www.amazon.com/dp/B01JQUTNPM

The Shocking Truth About Sexual Blackmail: The Secrets Cyber Scammers Don't Want You To Know - The World's Best Advice On How To Deal With Sexual Blackmailers

http://www.amazon.com/dp/B01IO1615Y

Dating Coach For Men: 9 Dating Success Secrets On How To Win The Woman Of Your Dreams

http://www.amazon.com/dp/B01IOHIPNY

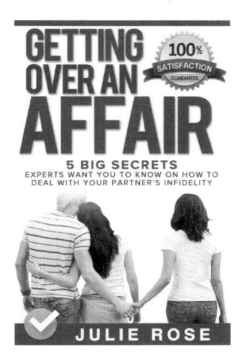

Getting Over An Affair: 5 Big Secrets Experts Want You To Know On How To Deal With Your Partner's Infidelity

http://www.amazon.com/dp/B01J7G5IVS

Productivity Secrets For Students: The Ultimate Guide To Improve Your Mental Concentration, Kill Procrastination, Boost Memory And Maximize Productivity In Study

http://www.amazon.com/dp/B01JS52UT6

12712754R00026

Printed in Germany
by Amazon Distribution
GmbH, Leipzig